Abandon body

Isla Greenwood

BookLeaf Publishing
India | USA | UK

Presentation by *BookLeaf Publishing*

Web: www.bookleafpub.com

E-mail: info@bookleafpub.com

ISBN: 978-93-5744-366-1

First edition 2022

'Now I'm sleepy but I will not sleep. I will take paper and pen and I will write. I sense an awful strength within me. I thought everything over yesterday already. It will be a story about a miracle worker who lives in our time and does not work miracles. He knows he is a miracle worker and could create any sort of miracle, but he does not do it. He is evicted from his apartment - he knows that we're he to just wave a finger the apartment would stay his, but he does not do it; he timidly vacates his apartment and lives outside of town in a shed. He can turn this old shed into a wonderful brick house, but he does not do it; he continues to live in the shed and in the end he dies, not having worked a single miracle in his life. I sit and wring my hands with joy. Sakerdon Mikhailovich will explode with envy. He thinks that I am no longer capable of writing a thing of genius. Quickly, quickly to work! Away with the sleep and laziness, I will write for eighteen hours straight!'

- Daniil Kharms

ACKNOWLEDGEMENT

My mother, brother, father, two grandmothers and the near 10 billion other members of my beautiful extended family of humanity.

'I think what motivates people is not great hate, but great love for people' Huey Newton

Accidental poetry and prose
I eat burnt bricks for breakfast
Instead of breakfast toast

Hope soup

All my fear is dissolving into
Hope soup
Every future image of a place I couldn't exist in
Becoming a river of permission

Every tension in my chest
Letting out a long deep breath.
Crack me up and open into a full belly laugh
at myself

Streams of green
Just pouring out of my chest my head my mouth
I'm the site of an abandoned fortress
Where nature has reclaimed its wealth

I'm all the tangled torture chamber
Burst open by the root
I'm the cracked, uncleaned windows
Shattered by new growth

And all my fear is dissolving
Into hope soup
And it's warming to my soul
And I hope it reaches you

Breathe

The walls I ran at for so long
Have let me run beyond
I'm everywhere all at once
And feel again like I belong

Why? Because I'm not playing this time
I don't care how fair or inevitable the game is
It just gave me a bad feeling - a tension
that cold hard loss of life you get in competition
but everyone's still breathing
I don't want that shit shaping my existence

I'm the crumbled empire in ruins
Shaken by the winds
I'm the new minds arriving
Just Beginning to settle in

And all my fear has evaporated
And rains down now in tears of laughter
And my body feels no pain anymore
Now I can see the way through any disaster

This chaos offered me the master key to open
And now I have
There is no going backwards
Only round in circles

Life spirals

Back home to slurp
My favourite flavour
Hope soup, I drink that shit in the bath.
And I hope you do too

Actors/self hypnosis/method
second to madness

All the forms we learn to love eventually trap us
The cracks start to appear
And we see that we're actors

What your soul really wants will spark you up to
get it
If it's just a fleeting image or idea
forget it

Sit in a circle and nurture / sisterhood / SIBLINGhood

Siblingf*****hood
Is to sit in a circle and nurture
The pains and the aches and the process
To listen actively
Interrupt accidentally
Choke up the words that before
We're hard to say

Siblingf*****hood
Has no ifs
No buts
No shoulds

It's a temple for possibility
Dreamt up by blooded fevers
That imagine what could be
What will be seen in
Swimming
And delivering
From the waters where
It's already happening

Siblingf*****hood
Is the food is the fat is the muddypuddle

The mothers cuddle
The too sweet smoothie
Too sticky pudding
The burnt shit stuck to the roof of your mouth
Siblingf*****hood is too much

Until again you fall in love
With the rage and the rawness
The browns and the purples
And the blood
Dried
Over and over again
Centuries through all of time
SIBLINGhood is not built or coppiced
Or carpented into existence
It's not even seeded as a motive for resistance

It just is

Like the rivers it comes forward at the beginning
The middle
And the end
When the worst is over
And when it's just beginning

Grows like a four leaf clover
When the soil's been turned over
Will not surrender
Unless it is to really do it

Give everything
Not just that we see as valuable bits
But all of it

Siblingf*****hood
Has got your heavy bricks
In the process
Shows you
You are
WEIGHTLESS

Doesn't shy away from the smell of your shit
Probabaly doesn't even notice it
Cause the love is so deep
It's so much more potent that what floats in the
surface

Breathe

Underneath all of it is the wordless
Drunk in a citrus juice like potion
Laced with salt and romance
Made by everyone who knows it

Drunk by those who

Loosen the ropes

Sisterhood goes looking at the cobwebs
And clears them away with the laughter

Fucking
SIBLING*******hood
Is the master
Of the craft of heating rooms with frozen rafters
SIBLINGhood is the silence
The buzz
The asymmetry
the imperfection

And the pulse

SIBLING*******hood is one of the rhythms
That will never
quiet down
on this earth

SIBLING*******hoodm

Flesh flower fire

There is a
Flesh
Flower
Fire inside

The house of the soul
Is not only in the thin mist just above the mind
But in the deep ick of your red and wet insides

It's a fragile piece of intricate technology
Easy to crush
I forget to acknowledge just
How tender a thing it becomes
Injected with wordless information from a
corporal journal of mine
Eternal meditation on your fleshy insides

Every shock, power trip
Trauma and falling deeper into it
Carved you into this shape
And every shake and release every latch onto
peace
And scream into the darkness of deep
Carved you into this shape

Every breath, every kiss
Every bite, loss and slip
Carved you into this
Every accident, passionate or drastic shift
Every drop in the mist
Carved you into this

You are the low slump of a blanket
Draped across the back of
Some Eternal mist
In the Rainforest
Lost again
Without a witness
Wet moss and synthetic fibre carpets
Soaked into your red landscapes

Your eyes lean back
Into your brain
Sink into sofa
language gone again
Visions visit and offer you a home
Red nests of muscle and bone
You are bloody
You'll soon be a carcass

All of these things
Carved you into this

All these fibre optic knowings
Ungraspable but essential showing
Intangible subliminal
gravity in denial

There will never be a book that could capture
every truth

That Carved you into this

Flesh
flower
Fire

But words are a small comfort that paint a
picture of

What carved you into this

Flesh
Flower
Fire

If only we could photosynthesise

Just imagine

Now that my love is gone everything feels like my lover

Now that my love is gone
Everything feels like my lover
The way the candle light flickers
Is the soft hands and tickles
The three minutes of pink sky in a sunrise
otherwise grey
Is the moment of inspiration
Even though my love is gone
There is love in this day

Mayo

BBQ the shit out of all your possessions
See what they look like when covered in ashes
Soak them in ketchup
And lick up the Mayo
The light looks so nice at the top of your halo

Can't help the other side of you

I can't help myself but to stoop over
There's another world I'm combing through
And another cover
My skin covered in butter
That I want to show you
I shave the zest off my lemon legs
It was a vision that I had
I chased it so hard
Ignoring the discomfort comfort would inflict

I bought a cat to this country
With eyes shot blue like the ancients
With a pale face
And green fur
And a smile that could make
 you
leave
You

OHe told you
Develop your mind like a nation
Grow your soul through an incantation

What bubbles up through me is a restlessness
And I'll never forget that way you talked through
me to yourself
We are not caged bodies of flesh
We are the bone marrow
The beasts need to eat you
To reimagine life
Itself

There is no flaw
My mother is divine but no saint
The others are within me
There's no such thing as
Separate

Your addiction to light will blind you
Sink into the depth of the darkness
There is a a pink and a red, an orange a gold and
a blueA shade by nature
That's one with you

Monotony, mediocrity, shame, taste and going
boldly
These are the shapes
That make a creature that will never hold me,
Your magnificence will never own me
For I pray only to a god who lives inside me

All of your patience

Has tested mine too
All your perfection put me to rest in thick goo
I set myself in resin to be pretty for you
But I'm disturbed now by the fact
That I can't move

I shatter the goo
And turn it to glass
I welcome 7 years of good luck
The mirrors mosaic perfect chaos
On the floor
Never before has it offered me
Such an accurate depiction
Of this universe

Gap in the market

19

Destroy the market
Engage in something that hasn't yet happened

In the arms of the earth

You can still fly if you try
Your wings are not what take you to the sky
It's your soul that soars
Higher than high
You can still fly if you try
You may have died
But in the arms of the earth
You are always
In life

Cuckoo

I listen to Chopin in the morning
With my grandmother
And try to inhabit
The years between us
All fifty of them
She has half a century more experience
But really what is the difference?
I pretending to be adult, responsible,
independent
Her wondering where her breakfast went
We catch each other
On parallel pages, indentical smiles, different
ages
Something chimes
And laughter spills out the top of us
We catch ourselves
 formed of the same material
Just each in a different disguise

Get you forget you

I remember a future
That looked like a flood
My memories crushed
Into what would become

I gathered the chaos
And sent it to seed
It grew into something
I never knew I would need

E - home

Everywhere I go
Is home
Everyone I know
Is home
Every eye I look into
Is one of my own
Everywhere I go
Is home

uncertainty

Uncertainty grants you the freedom
To challenge all of your assumptions

untitled 1

If I am anything
I am connection
If I'm going anywhere
It's to sediment

untitled 2

Every situation
Demands something different
The only way to be
Is present

pink walls

Where are you taking me
Place with the pink dissolving walls
This tunnel ahead is faint
But I can't get it out of my head

What's the most important thing?
I had a sex dream
I felt everything
Collateral damage to all my illusions
And I no longer have insurance

Don't have any pockets on my skin
To store things in

So now I can live in my life
Not just inhabit the space
Now I can feel all the light
And how the dark illuminates
I can't ignore the charge
That pushes on my muscles
I have no choice but to move
Exactly as they offer

My mind has never been ahead

It's my bones and my flesh and my blood
That tell me what is next

I'm finally
Meeting all parts of this nature
Just let them run
Experimentation
Trial and error

You first allow yourself to be
And then you become

Gratitude

Nature

Thank you for being the safest space holder for
surrender
Thank you for filling my being with humour
Thank you for making me an embodiment of
firasha
Thank you for saving me in days when I don't
care
Thank you for bringing me out to breathe
All flair
Thank you for filling my lungs with a breeze
Thank you for bringing me down to my knees
Thank you for soaking up all of my hate

PAUSE

Thank you for holding me down when I wanted
to jump
That you for jumping me up when you saw I
was stuck
Thank you for telling me tales that I made and
forgot
Thank you for pulling me into your heart

Thank you for pushing me out into art
Thank you for holding me up in the street
Thank you for bringing me back to the start
Thank you for time and time again bringing me
Back to your nature
Saviour
Tree
Green
The things I've seen as against you I lean
The things I've been with you as I've breathed
The wonders uncovered
Secrets discovered
Spiders, cycles, webs connected
Life resurrected
Death celebrated
As it turns we all witness
Your grace, your patience, the way you hold us
up
Your rhythm
Your hunger
And your understanding us

Mother Nature old wise tree
Thank you for showing me how you can be free
When you're locked behind bars in a park
Freedom is contextual
How it textures our lives we decide
That's essential

Holy

The moon is always full
And you are always whole

Oil angels

They sat at the top of the plastic ice cream cone
most days
Someone stole and rolled away the flavours
So they became them
From a distance they looked like two birds
Circled up in a nest
Featherless
But restful
And that's exactly how they felt
They'd arrived finally
And in some way it matched what they'd
imagined
But they could never had known the details
The taste of the air was inescapable
It poured in through every pore in their skin
And it was like they'd breathed in the halos
Of oil angels

www.ingramcontent.com/pod-product-compliance
Lightning Source LLC
LaVergne TN
LVHW010932200726
843509LV00013B/2192